ENJOY PLAYING
GUITAR SOLOS

Twenty progressive pieces for the early grades

DEBBIE CRACKNELL

Illustrations by Adrian Barclay

Music Department
OXFORD UNIVERSITY PRESS
Oxford and New York

Oxford University Press, Great Clarendon Street, Oxford OX2 6DP, England
Oxford University Press Inc., 198 Madison Avenue, New York, NY 10016, USA

Oxford is a trade mark of Oxford University Press

© Oxford University Press 1998

Olé José

Give this piece a lively Spanish feel (*allegretto* means 'fairly fast and lively').
Strum where indicated (↑↓) in the direction of the arrows, being very careful
to hit only the first three strings.

Printed in Great Britain
OXFORD UNIVERSITY PRESS, MUSIC DEPARTMENT, GREAT CLARENDON STREET, OXFORD OX2 6DP

Musette

A Musette is a type of French bagpipe which was popular in the 17th and 18th centuries. Bagpipes make a 'drone'—a continuous note heard throughout the piece—which is imitated here by the bass A. Use a rest stroke for the beginning and ending sections, and free strokes in the middle (bars 9–16). *Pont.* (or 'ponticello') means play near the bridge; *nat.* is back to the natural sound.

Sussex carol

Like *Musette*, this uses a drone bass at the beginning. It could be accompanied by a small drum, which would give the piece a traditional early English flavour; the rhythm ♩. ♩ ♪ will work for most of the piece, but bars 16 and 17 would need the simpler rhythm of ♩. ♩. ♩. | ♩. ♩. to fit in with the change of time signature.

Allegretto

English Traditional

Lullaby

Give this a gentle feel (*tranquillo* means 'calm and gentle'). Bring out the
melody line where indicated by the accents (>). Take care to hold all the
dotted minims and tied notes for their full value. ❦ is a 'comma pause'—take
a slight pause before the next phrase. *Gliss.* (or 'glissando') means slide the
4th finger from the G to the B.

Pepé's sombrero

This is a typical Spanish sounding piece using running passages in the bass and repeated top Es (bars 17–24) which are found in much Flamenco music. Keep the two-note chords in the first and last sections quieter than the bass lines.

Ding dong! merrily on high

This is an old French tune which is still popular today as a Christmas carol.
Vivace means lively, so aim for a feeling of two in a bar. Be careful to alternate
'i' and 'm' fingers of the right hand throughout the piece; the thumb of course
keeps to the bass line.

Robin's revel

This piece is in the style of the lute music common in Elizabethan times. Aim for a speed of ♩. = 68 (this metronome mark shows the number of indicated notes per minute). Keep the dotted rhythms very crisp, and use *ponticello* (see *Musette*) where shown to give this piece its early music feel.

Coconut corn

Use the expression signs (particularly the accents) to keep this piece in a lively Caribbean style. Take care to slide the D chord shape in bar 30 up two frets in bar 31 so the right-hand arpeggio can then be played as normal. End with a short, sharp chord, indicated by the staccato dots (𝄽) above and below the notes.

A strange dream

Keep the speed moderate (*moderato*), and give the piece a calm dream-like quality. Five beats to a bar is an unusual time signature (perhaps this dream was *very* strange). Use the accents in bars 9, 10, 13, and 14 to change the emphasis on to the first and fourth beats. When you see a pause sign ( ) on the last note of a piece, pause slightly *before* the note to create the best effect.

14

Carnival in the rain

The South American rhythm is lively, but the minor key gives this piece a slightly sad feel. Note the *meno mosso* (less movement) in the last two bars, and play slower. Enjoy the very high A at the end—it's on the 17th fret of the first string!

The foggy dew

This is a straightforward English folk tune, but watch the rhythm in bar 14.
Care with the left-hand fingering will help to keep the melody line smooth.

English Traditional

The willow tree

The phrase lines (long lines above a group of bars) help to divide a piece into 'sentences'. Take a 'breath'—a very slight pause—at the end of a phrase, and it will help to give the music shape.

17

Apache dance

There are some high positions in this one! However, everything fits the hand well if you keep to the given left-hand fingering and string numbers. *Tambora* means that while holding the Em chord you hit strings 4, 5, and 6 very near the bridge with the right-hand thumb.

Skye boat song

Like *Musette,* this Scottish tune has a drone in the first and last sections, here to imitate the sound of the Scottish bagpipe. This bass G makes the piece more difficult than it looks, although it stays in first position. Hold the G with the 3rd finger throughout bars 1–12 and 21–32, and use the 4th finger for all the second string Ds.

Traditional Scottish

Athena's dance

Written in a Greek style, this piece uses repeated semiquavers (AA CC BB etc.) which are common in music for the bouzouki, a long-necked metal-strung instrument usually played with a plectrum. As usual, use alternate right hand fingers 'i' and 'm' on the melody line. Note the change of key from A minor to D minor (B♭ in the key signature) at bar 17. The sign ⌇ is a 'mordent' (which is optional here): play the main note, then the note above (in the scale), then the main note again (CDC in bar 7, FGF in bar 23), all very rapidly and all slurred.

On the high plateau

The diamond shaped notes are harmonics, produced by touching the string lightly with the left hand exactly above the metal of the fret indicated and plucking normally with the right, which causes a ringing effect. Strings are indicated in circles, and fret numbers as normal figures. The small note in bars 5 and 9 is an *acciaccatura* (a 'crushed' note): play it on the beat with a fast slur to the main note. Let the tied semibreve Es ring on like a church bell heard in the distance.

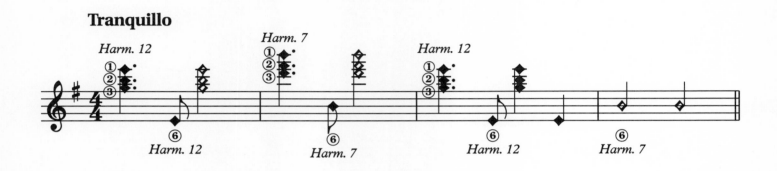

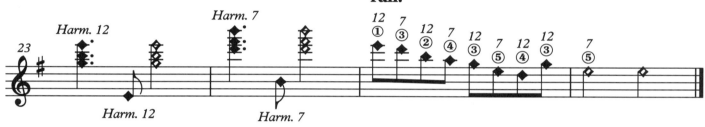

Daffodil waltz

The waltz was a popular dance in the 19th century, especially in Vienna. Aim for at least ♩. = 50 to keep the dance moving. A little emphasis on the first beat of each bar will keep your imaginary dancers in step.

Nashville Nick

This has the style of American 'country' music and needs to sound laid back! The piece may look simple on the page, but the F chord at bars 11, 12, 27, and 28 will take practice. Use the right-hand thumb for all the bass notes (the melody), and strum lightly with 'i' down/up, across the first three strings on all the chords. *Simile* means 'the same': carry on strumming down/up throughout the piece. *Yee-haa!*

Moondust

Lento misterioso means slow and mysterious. This piece is much easier than it looks as it consists mainly of sliding left-hand fingers 2 and 3 together up and down the fingerboard on strings ① and ②. Slow right down at the end with a *pianissimo* (**pp** = very soft) last chord.

Those homework blues!

We all know the feeling! When you see 'jazz 8ths' or 'swing rhythm' (♫ = ♪³♪)
indicated at the beginning of a piece, play all the ♫ rhythms long/short. The
acciaccaturas in bars 1, 3, 5, and 7 are to be played with a slide to the main note;
this is indicated by a straight slide line as well as the curved slur line.

rit.

Printed and bound in Great Britain by
Caligraving Limited Thetford Norfolk

CONTENTS